The Coaching ADVANTAGE in New-age WORKPLACES

The Coaching ADVANTAGE in New-age WORKPLACES

Manjula Banerji

Worldwide Published by
Pendown Press

PENDOWN PRESS LLP

An ISO 9001 & ISO 14001 Certified Co.,

Regd. Office: 3767A, Kanhaiya Nagar,

Tri Nagar, Delhi-110035

Ph.: 8130886000, 9650072927

E-mail: info@pendownpress.com

Branch Office: 1A/2A, 20, Hari Sadan, Ansari Road,

Daryaganj, New Delhi-110002

Ph.: 011-45794768

Website: PendownPress.com

Edition: 2025

Price: ₹ 299

ISBN: 978-93-6338-676-1

Layout and Cover Designed by Pendown Graphics Team

Printed and Bound in India by Thomson Press India Ltd.

AUTHOR'S NOTE

To every professional who chose growth over comfort,

To the leaders who embraced change and became the change,

To the seekers of clarity, purpose, and higher performance,

To the brave hearts who believed in the power of transformation,

This is for you —

May your journey always be guided
by intention, insight, and impact.

TABLE OF CONTENTS

1 PREFACE

Deep down, do you believe senior professionals in your organization need to be more agile, ace their performance, build their personal brand, elevate their leadership competencies, and nurture talent to propel exponential growth of your organization?

Yes or No?

If you've ever felt the frustration of seeing potential go untapped… if you've questioned whether your top leaders are truly ready for what's next… if you've sensed that something needs to shift—but weren't sure what or how, then you're not alone.

As the CHRO/Business Leader of your organization, I want to let you know that your search ends here. What lies ahead is not just a framework; it's a new lens to view leadership, talent, and transformation. It's the kind of shift that turns stagnation into momentum and good leaders into great ones.

The Power of Transformative Transitions is revealed!

Let's begin this journey of change not in theory, but in action.

❖ ❖ ❖ ❖

2 ACKNOWLEDGEMENTS

Whatever I have achieved in life would have been impossible without the support of my parents. They've taught me values, ethics, diligence, and perseverance. The wings I have today would not have been possible without them.

To my husband, Mr. Sankha Banerji, who has stood by me in every situation. You've not only shared my dreams but have made sacrifices to bring them to fruition. Thank you for being my calm in chaos, my biggest cheerleader, and my partner in every sense.

To my daughter Pallavi, who is the source of my happiness and inspiration. Lots of love!

My heartfelt gratitude to all my mentors and guides, who have shown me light and direction in times of adversity and uncertainty.

To our clients, who have shared their experiences and knowledge with us during this journey. Thank you for trusting us and being our inspiration.

A special acknowledgement goes to Dinesh Verma and his wonderful team at Pendown Press. From the initial concept to the final manuscript, their support and expertise have made this book possible.

And finally, to all my loved ones who have been with me on this journey—thank you for your unwavering support, encouragement, and affection. Even if your names are not mentioned, you always hold a special place in my heart.

Without the support of all of you, it would not have been possible for me to move forward with confidence.

❖ ❖ ❖ ❖

3 About The Author

My Story

A Legacy of Expertise and Leadership

I am Manjula Banerji, a Fellow Member of the Institute of Chartered Accountants of India and an accredited Professional Coach from the International Coaching Federation, USA. With four decades of corporate experience as a former Audit & Assurance Partner and Board Member of Deloitte Haskins & Sells LLP, my journey has been shaped by a passion for nurturing talent, inspiring leadership, and fostering sustainable growth. Over the years, I have had the privilege of working with brilliant minds and witnessing the transformative power of mentorship and intentional leadership.

The Beginning:
Balancing Work and Motherhood

Early in my career, working in a professional services firm gave me the opportunity to connect with people. As I scaled up to a managerial role, I began overseeing a team of young professionals, mentoring them through their formative years. At the same time, I became a mother to a baby girl—an experience that made nurturing, caring, and protecting my child central to my life. This dual role of mother and manager became a defining moment in my life, one that taught me the true essence of empathy, resilience, and collaboration. It shaped how I empowered others in the workplace—with compassion, strength, and authenticity.

Caring and Connecting: Building Relationships at Work

At work, I extended the same nurturing mindset to my team members. I cared for them, connected deeply, and collaborated to help them find solutions to their challenges. Over time, this approach became an integral part of my leadership style—one focused on empathy, guidance, and support. It wasn't just about driving performance; it was about building trust and helping individuals evolve into the best version of themselves.

The Talent Challenge: Observing Gaps in Development

As I grew within the firm and took on the role of a partner, I began to observe recurring talent challenges both within my firm and the industry at large. Issues such as employee burnout, high attrition, short attention spans, and limited investment in personal learning and development, especially among senior professionals, stood out to me. These challenges weren't just statistics; they were signals calling for urgent and meaningful intervention. These gaps became central to my work, sparking a desire to bring change.

Creating a Culture of Coaching and Mentoring

I worked diligently to establish a culture of executive coaching and mentoring in my firm with the support of the Business Leader and colleagues. I coached and mentored professionals at various levels, helping them develop self-awareness and emphasizing the importance of personal growth. This initiative went beyond skill-building, it laid the foundation for a more empowered, resilient, and future-ready workforce. It also played a key role in succession planning, with many professionals eventually stepping confidently into partnership roles.

Overcoming Challenges With Compassion

The senior professionals I coached were deeply committed to client service and often struggled to prioritize coaching sessions. With compassion, I followed up with them regularly and adjusted my schedule to accommodate their needs. My persistence and understanding helped shift their beliefs and behaviors, eventually leading to profound personal and professional growth.

Transformative Results: Impacting Lives and Careers

Over months of consistent coaching, these professionals began noticing significant improvements in their interactions with team members, clients, and even their families. They became more solution-oriented, handled challenges effectively, and exhibited better emotional control. Through coaching and mentoring, I had the privilege of supporting numerous professionals, contributing to the creation of a more empowered, self-aware, and resilient workforce.

A New Chapter: Building My Coaching Practice

Post my retirement from Deloitte, I embarked on a new journey—establishing my own Executive Coaching & Mentoring practice. My mission is to continue empowering professionals to grow, thrive, and lead with authenticity, empathy, and self-awareness. For me, this is not just a career—it is a calling to build leaders who lead from within.

❖ ❖ ❖ ❖

MY MOTTO
GROWTH THROUGH DISCOMFORT

"Be comfortable with the uncomfortable to propel your growth engine."

4 PURPOSE OF THE BOOK

In my corporate career spanning 4 decades, I have witnessed numerous professionals getting stuck in their careers, unable to elevate themselves to higher levels within their organizations, despite their talent and dedication.

I was deeply motivated to write this book for such professionals, to share valuable insights, practical perspectives, and my own lived experiences of working closely with them. Over the years, I have helped many navigate self-doubt, overcome limiting beliefs, and move past the internal barriers that held them back.

Through the **Transformative Transitions Framework**, I guide readers on a journey of awakening self-awareness, conducting honest assessments, taking meaningful action, and ultimately achieving success not just in their careers, but in their personal growth as well.

This book is a reflection of real challenges and real breakthroughs. It is written with the intent to spark introspection, provoke clarity, and inspire movement. Whether you are at a turning point, feeling stagnant, or simply seeking to lead more effectively, this book offers tools and pathways to reimagine what is possible.

My hope is that every professional who reads this finds renewed energy, greater conviction, and the courage to take that next step forward with intention and purpose.

5 BENEFIT FOR THE READERS

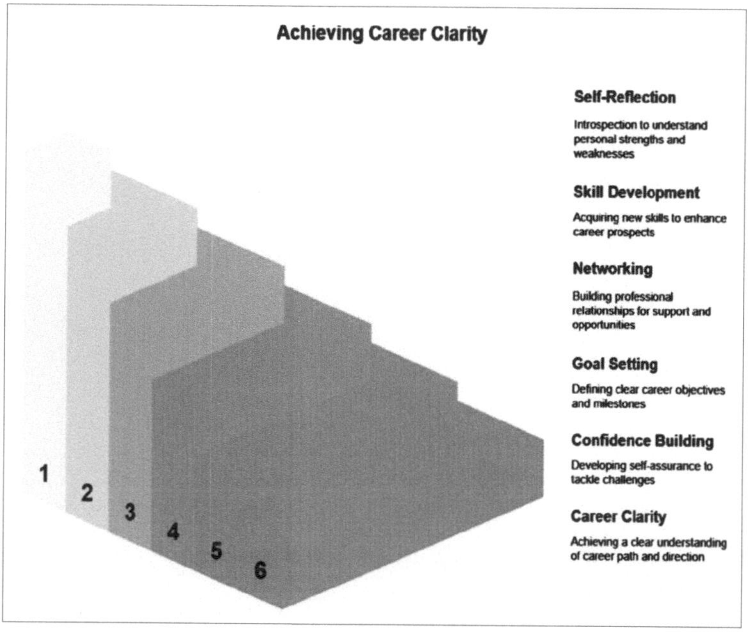

You will learn what mistakes to avoid in your career and save valuable time, energy, and money.

You will learn the methods of elevating yourself and navigating your career progression with greater clarity and confidence.

You will discover new perspectives and hidden opportunities that can accelerate your growth and take you to the next level.

You will gain practical ideas to build and strengthen your personal brand, making you conspicuous in a competitive environment.

This book will act as a trusted mentor, guiding you to grow, succeed, and create a meaningful impact in both your professional and personal life.

❖ ❖ ❖ ❖

TRANSFORMATIVE TRANSITIONS FRAMEWORK

The Transformative Transitions Framework Comprises of 5 Building Blocks:

The 5As' Are Summarized Below:

- Awakening Awareness
- Assessments
- Actions
- Absorption
- Achievements

Each one of the above is discussed in detail.

❖ ❖ ❖ ❖

6 AWAKENING AWARENESS

Awakening awareness is like a wake-up call from a deep slumber. It awakens a human being from a mechanical way of life to a magnetic way of life. Awareness sharpens our perception of the way we perceive ourselves viz-a-viz our outside environment, composed of people in our personal relationships, in the community, at our workplace, etc. It helps us see things we might otherwise overlook, such as our hidden strengths, unrecognized patterns, and untapped potential.

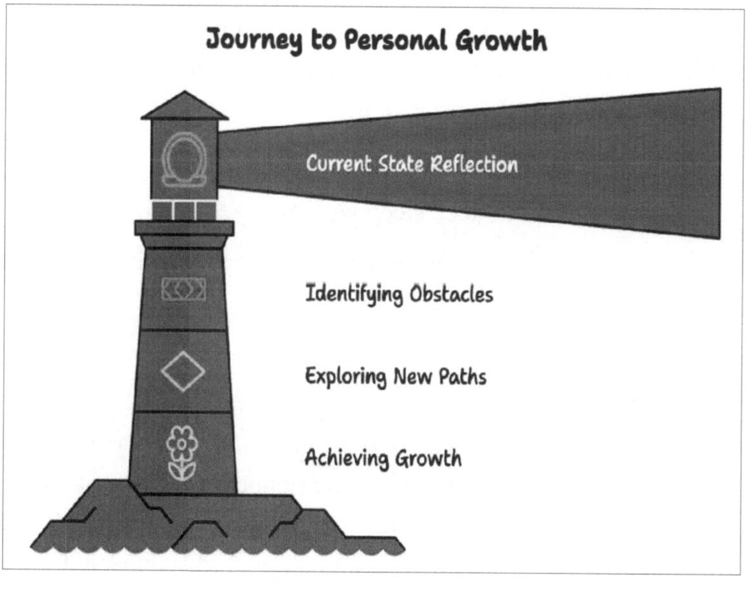

Awareness facilitates deep internal reflection and introspection regarding our current state in life. It shines a light on what has been keeping us stuck, while opening up new paths for growth and improvement. It helps us move from internal darkness towards the light, as we get insights and fresh perspectives regarding the realm of possibilities to reach our desired state in life and make a meaningful impact. We move from a fixed mindset to a growth mindset and take our first step towards our liberation from negative thoughts, negative self-talk and limiting beliefs.

In our everyday lives, we have numerous opportunities to change the trajectory of our lives. Every living moment, there is an opportunity. You may ask, *"How?"* I cannot find it. *Show me where it is*?

Calm down. I will reveal the secret in a moment.

Every moment has an opportunity, but you might miss it because you're not aware. When you become truly present, even ordinary things start to show their true value.

You may ask again—*How? Why? How come?*

It is because we are in deep sleep with our eyes open!

We are living our lives mechanically and not magnetically. Being awakeningly aware is a wake-up call from our deep slumber!

For the first time, we become aware of how exactly we are living our lives.

When we live mechanically, we fall into a **'default syndrome'**. In this state, we stop experiencing the richness of life through the beautiful gifts we are born with—our five senses, our mind, our heart, and our body. We function on autopilot, disconnected from the present moment.

The default syndrome is hardwired into our brain. It demands no extra effort, which is why it feels so easy and comfortable. But this comfort zone slowly makes us dull, predictable, and uninspired. We repeat the same patterns of behavior, expecting something new yet nothing new ever comes.

To create something fresh and meaningful, we must move our inner gears from mechanical to magnetic. This shift is not just a mindset change, it is an invitation to live fully, to feel deeply, and to respond consciously.

This is where magic is waiting to enter our lives.

Are you willing to make the switch?

This switch requires complete surrender from your side for the change to manifest in the entire spectrum of your life.

Are you ready?

Let us move forward. Once we become aware, we begin to unlock and unleash our limitless creative energy. We start engaging fully with life using the incredible combination of our five senses, mind, heart, and body. That is when we truly begin to live, not just exist.

We are able to see the Wonders of the Universe by being observant of our surroundings. This will be the first step towards utilizing our boundless powers of observation both in our personal and professional environments. It helps us remain alert to our behaviors and attitudes towards people, whether they are family members, colleagues at the workplace, or individuals in the community.

We begin to recognize our emotional triggers in relationships and learn to respond with maturity instead of reacting impulsively. Reactivity is a mechanical response, but awareness brings presence and choice. This facilitates mature interactions in our personal and professional relationships and elevates us in a personal way.

As we awaken our awareness, we begin to feel the rhythm of our own breath. We notice the blooming flowers, the swaying trees, and the gentle breeze caressing our face. We start to truly admire the bounties of the Universe. We begin to enjoy the simple, profound gift of sight.

We feel alive – truly alive!

Do you want to experience it?

Then go ahead and take the first step towards building your awareness.

Being aware can liberate you from the monotony of daily routine. It opens up a new dimension of living, filled with presence, appreciation, and joy.

When we use our ears to listen to people and use our voice to respond with full awareness, it has the potential to elevate the quality of our communication with family, colleagues at work, and in the community.

Our interactions are more meaningful and binding with each other. We can appreciate warmth in our relationships and enlarge the areas in which we operate, become more empathetic, and expand our viewpoints about our feelings and beliefs.

This shift in awareness is not just a personal transformation; it has a ripple effect.

As we become more mindful and centered, we inspire others to do the same. Our energy shifts, and the people around us sense that change. In this way, awareness is not just a tool for personal elevation but a quiet force that uplifts the collective spirit of every space we walk into.

We are able to observe ourselves closely and identify our negative self-talk, limiting beliefs, and our fears, which are holding us back from achieving our true potential.

I hope you can now start appreciating the criticality of awareness in your lives.

Awareness can facilitate the synchronization of your mind, heart, body, and five senses to find solutions to your challenges and live purposeful lives.

Being aware each moment requires a lot of effort, dedication, and perseverance. It is not always easy but the transformation it brings is worth it. *So, are you ready to begin this journey of inner awakening?*

❖ ❖ ❖ ❖

7 ASSESSMENTS

Once self-awareness has set in, the next step is self-assessment.

Some indicators include:

- Personal Health
- Wisdom
- Conviction
- Tolerance
- Youthfulness
- Passion
- Courage
- Victory

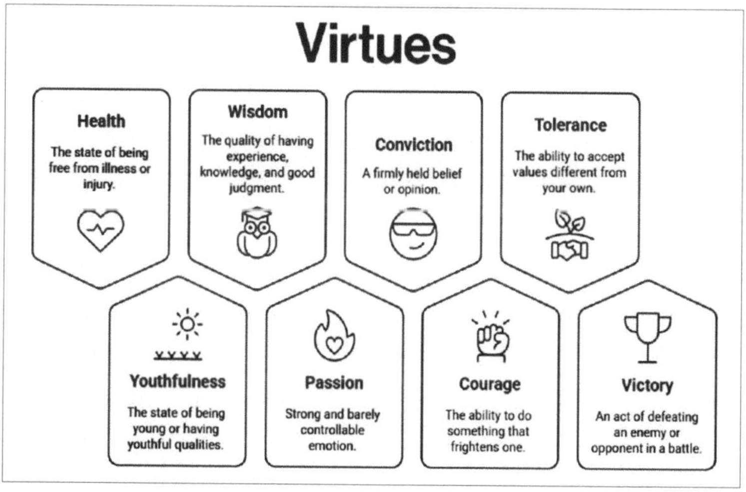

The above indicators are illustrative, not exhaustive. Let us discuss the above indicators in some detail:

Your health is the prime point to begin with in the self- introspection journey. When the body is functioning optimally, the mind also finds clarity. A sound body supports a sound mind, and together they serve as the launchpad for deeper awareness.

Leading a healthy life will work to your advantage. You may not be able to work your hardest if your health is compromised. **Energy is the currency of action** and without health, our ambitions remain ideas that never see the light of day.

Maintaining a youthful spirit can help you to traverse adversity and be solution oriented. This spirit doesn't come from age but from attitude, the ability to bounce back, stay curious, and believe in possibility.

Wisdom may mean to manifest our cognitive abilities, which helps one to move from a lesser self to a larger self. It's the shift from reaction to reflection, from compulsiveness to consciousness.

Passion can invigorate our commitment to make lives purposeful, satisfying, and create happiness. It adds intensity to our intentions and brings color to even the dullest routines.

Conviction facilitates living our lives ethically and serves as a compass to navigate the direction of our lives. It gives us the inner strength to stand for what is right, even when it is not easy.

Courage enables us to live compassionately and show genuine concern towards the welfare of others in the environment. Courage is not just boldness; it is the strength to be kind in a harsh world.

Tolerance helps us to be broad-minded and make others comfortable and at ease. It's about accepting diversity not just in people, but also in thoughts, opinions, and approaches.

Living life with compassion and ethics fuels good health, youthfulness, wisdom, passion, conviction, courage and tolerance and facilitates our victory. Victory here is not conquest over others, but a triumph over our own lower tendencies.

Self - assessment is akin to a self- diagnostic tool and facilitates our attention to an inward focus. We are alone with ourselves. In the beginning, it can feel unfamiliar and sound strange. As you delve into an inward journey, it is a surreal feeling of newness, freshness, and excitement. Your curiosity is piqued. Over time, it grows into a journey of self- discovery.

Self-assessment facilitates our learning and development skills, as it makes us aware of our strengths and areas for development. It helps us to take proactive steps in our growth journey. We can make sound choices to leverage our strengths in both personal and professional environments. Manifesting our strengths at the workplace creates a realm of possibilities for advancement in our careers.

Think of self-assessment as the mirror that doesn't just reflect who you are but who you are becoming. It encourages honesty, courage, and responsibility, while nurturing a vision for who you wish to grow into.

Organizations employ various methodologies for performance evaluation of their professionals on a quarterly, half yearly, or annual basis.

Professionals who assess themselves are in a more empowered space—it's no longer about being assessed by others, but being aligned with oneself. It facilitates confident, meaningful discussions with assessors and helps individuals articulate their progress with clarity, authenticity, and purpose.

When you step into a review with self-awareness, you no longer feel like a passenger in your career, you become the driver.

Do you feel better placed in life through the awakening awareness and the self - assessment process?

What has opened up for you? Are you feeling empowered and more in control over your life?

Pause for a moment. You have come a long way from being on autopilot to awakening. From surviving to self-reflecting. From wandering to walking with intent. That itself is a quiet revolution.

Let us move forward. *Ready?*

The awakening awareness and self-assessment exercises were to prime you for the action piece.

❖ ❖ ❖ ❖

8 ACTIONS

Welcome to the world of executive coaching and mentoring, wherein a realm of opportunities for self- transformation will be unveiled to you!

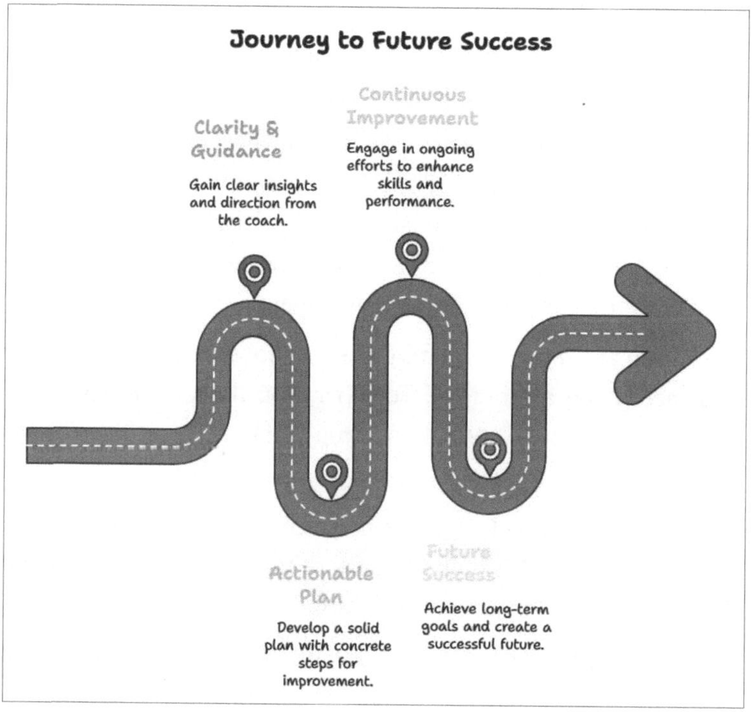

Curious? Ready?

In simple terms, executive coaching is a dialogue between the executive coach and a client. In this process, the coach listens to the client's challenges, asks powerful questions, and provides a safe space for introspection. This enables the client to get insights and perspectives and arrive at solutions on their own. The goal is to help the client view challenges as stepping stones for personal growth and transformation. Through this journey, the client's mindset shifts from a fixed mindset to a growth mindset. The focus transitions from being problem-oriented to being solution-oriented.

Imagine this shift as a key unlocking countless doors of possibility, each leading to your next level of achievement.

A change in mindset opens up new pathways and empowers the client to become agile, elevate their performance, demonstrate ownership, and take responsibility for nurturing talent within their organization. It nurtures a sense of leadership that thrives on growth, self-awareness, and empowerment.

The coach assists you in setting clear, actionable goals tailored to your needs and aspirations. Together, you'll chart out strategies and outline concrete actions that you'll take to meet these goals within a set time frame.

But here's the secret: the true power of coaching doesn't lie in the strategy alone. It's in the consistent application of insights and the accountability that accompanies it.

By embracing the guidance of an executive coach, you gain not just clarity but a solid, actionable plan for continuous improvement—both personally and professionally. You're not just achieving goals; you're crafting the very blueprint for your future success.

Benefits of Executive Coaching

An Executive Coach employs a personalized, holistic approach tailored specifically to your needs. It's not a one-size-fits-all method but rather a customized coaching intervention that focuses on you, your strengths, your goals, and your aspirations. The coach encourages you to embrace your full potential and deepen your self-awareness across various dimensions of life.

The coaching process is led by *you* – you decide the agenda and the outcome for the coaching session. This encourages your authenticity and self-awareness.

Coaching sessions facilitate alignment with your core values and promote deep introspection. The coach helps you reflect on your values and identify the actions necessary to align your life with those values. Through this, you gain clarity, focus, and direction in both personal and professional matters.

More than just professional growth, coaching enhances your resilience, stress tolerance, and emotional intelligence.

By nurturing these skills, you're better equipped to face challenges with composure and agility, turning obstacles into opportunities.

The benefits of executive coaching extend beyond you to your organization as well. Enhanced employee engagement, leadership, productivity, and communication are key organizational gains from coaching. As you grow, so does the team you lead.

In the coaching sessions, you will be able to create development plans tailored to your strengths and improvement areas. You can also apply the learnings for the development of your team members.

Coaching sessions will develop your critical leadership abilities such as decision-making, emotional intelligence, and conflict resolution.

Your coach will boost your confidence and transform your fixed mindset to a growth mindset, building your resilience and leadership competencies.

Through constructive feedback, your coach will help you engage in self-reflection, refine your skills, and continuously improve, ensuring that you're always moving forward in your journey.

A crucial aspect of executive coaching is the safe space it provides for navigating the emotional challenges that come with leadership. With consistent support, your coach will track your progress, ensuring you stay on course to meet your goals.

(Source: Coach Mentoring Ltd, UK)

I want to share the benefits of executive coaching & mentoring backed by research findings:

It's important to note that the return on investment (ROI) from coaching should be measured not only in financial terms but also qualitatively, through the growth and transformation experienced by individuals and organizations.

Coaching ROI and Its Impact: Key Insights

- **High ROI:** Executive coaching can yield up to 7X returns, boosting revenue and profits significantly.
- **Financial Gains:** Coaching cultures see up to 87% higher net profit margins and a 225% average growth in five-year revenue.

- **Employee Engagement:** 72% of employees report increased engagement as a result of coaching, and 78% of executives view it as a valuable tool for growth.
- **Broad Appreciation:** Both senior executives (78%) and employees (73%) recognize the value of executive coaching & mentoring.

(Sources: ICF, BetterUp, Forbes.com)

Building Coaching Cultures in Organizations

- **Organizational Benefits:** Coaching cultivates an environment that boosts employee retention, engagement, and financial outcomes. It helps develop a workforce that's more invested and motivated, driving organizational success.
- **Proven Success:** AstraZeneca, a global leader in healthcare, saw significant improvements in trust and team morale as a result of its coaching programs. These outcomes translated into a more collaborative and high-performing workforce.
- **Team Dynamics:** Promotes a culture of trust, open dialogue, and collaboration. By fostering healthy communication and team cohesion, it helps organizations overcome barriers and build stronger, more effective teams.

(Source: ICF Human Capital Institute)

Empowering Employees Across Generations

- **Bridging Age Gaps:** Coaching is an invaluable tool for bridging generational divides, particularly helping Gen-Z employees build confidence, foster trust, and improve retention within the workplace. It empowers them to develop the necessary skills to excel in their roles.

- **Leadership Development:** Executive coaching enhances leadership skills, increasing productivity and employee engagement. It equips individuals with the tools to lead with clarity, compassion, and vision.
- **Enhanced Team Dynamics:** Promotes a culture of trust, encouraging open dialogue and teamwork. As teams grow stronger and more united, they can better tackle challenges and achieve shared goals.
- **Mentorship Focus:** Gen - Z employees increasingly prefer mentorship over traditional authoritarian management styles. This shift highlights the growing importance of coaching to drive career growth, build relationships, and ensure workplace success.

(Sources: Workforce Institute at Kronos Inc., ICF Human Capital Institute)

Measuring the Impact of Executive Coaching & Mentoring

- **ROI Metrics:** The return on investment from executive coaching is measurable through key metrics such as employee retention, revenue growth, and behavioral changes as reflected in surveys.
- **Key Performance Indicators:** Signs of successful coaching include improvements in teamwork, leadership development, and overall performance. These indicators reflect a tangible shift in both individual and organizational outcomes.
- **Trust- Building:** Establishing and maintaining trust is a vital marker of effective coaching. The ability to create a trusting environment is crucial for sustained growth and long-term success.

(Source: Kinkajouconsulting.com)

Strategies for Transformative Executive Coaching & Mentoring

- **Strength: Based Development** Building a positive organizational culture starts with focusing on strengths. Coaching fosters motivation by encouraging individuals to harness their unique talents and leverage them for personal and professional growth.
- **Effective Coaching Practices:** Executive coaches employ strategies such as curiosity, acknowledging values, addressing negative self-talk, and challenging limiting beliefs. These practices help individuals gain new perspectives, overcome barriers, and unlock their full potential.
- **Empowerment:** Coaching empowers individuals to take action, implement solutions, and be accountable for their growth. It instills a sense of ownership and responsibility for both personal and organizational success.
- **Problem Solving:** Coaching is also a powerful tool for addressing issues proactively. It encourages individuals to approach challenges with a solution-oriented mindset, fostering resilience and innovation.

(Source: Coachingmastery.com)

Sustaining a Culture of Continuous Improvement: The ultimate benefit of executive coaching and mentoring is its ability to create a self-sustaining culture of continuous improvement. As individuals embrace growth mindsets and actively engage in their development, they influence others, creating a ripple effect throughout the organization. Over time, this culture leads to a more adaptable, resilient, and innovative workforce that thrives on change and continuously elevates performance across the board.

I want to bust some myths regarding executive coaching:

- **Myth:** Executive coaching is only for fixing problems
- **Reality:** Executive coaching is not just about fixing problems. Its true value is in preventing problems and enabling you to spot issues even before they arise. It facilitates personal growth, continuous learning, and managing risks in an effective way.
- **Myth:** Executive coaching is a sign of incompetence in a leader
- **Reality:** On the contrary, executive coaching is a sign of strength, self- awareness, and emotional intelligence. Leaders who recognize the value of continuous learning and development actively seek a coach to support them in refining their skills and overcoming obstacles.
- **Myth:** Executive coaching is time-consuming and disruptive
- **Reality:** Coaching requires time and commitment, but by its nature, it is a flexible process that can be tailored to your schedule. It is a necessary and strategic investment in yourself that yields exponential returns in clarity, focus, and performance.

(Source: Rachel Collar - HR Rockstar)

- **Myth:** Executive coaching is an unorganized sector
- **Reality:** Executive coaching is an increasingly structured and credible profession. Reputable coaches hold certifications from globally recognized bodies like the International Coaching Federation (ICF), USA. These credentials ensure ethical standards, coaching rigor, and measurable outcomes.

Executive coaching is rapidly gaining recognition in India as a business imperative. Numerous large and mid-sized organizations now engage certified executive coaches to support their senior leaders, mid-level managers, and emerging talent, enhancing organizational learning and leadership development at every level.

- **Myth:** Executive coaching may not yield tangible outcomes.
- **Reality:** Executive coaching is akin to a GPS, which puts you on the right track in your journey of self- development and growth. If you exhibit genuine interest and time in your growth journey, a coach can be your best friend. Your coach can facilitate your blossoming as a person, and you can elevate to magnificent levels in your life. Become curious, and a coach can create a paradigm shift in mindset.

Why Now Is the Best Time to Embrace Coaching

In an era defined by constant change and complexity, leaders can no longer rely solely on experience. What worked yesterday might not work tomorrow. Executive coaching equips you with the agility and mindset required to lead in uncertain times. It's not just about keeping up; it's about staying ahead. The leaders of tomorrow are those who choose to evolve today.

❖ ❖ ❖ ❖

9 ABSORPTION

During the coaching sessions with an Executive Coach and after completion of the coaching sessions, you are going through a transformative journey, learning new behaviours, expanding mindset and new ways of looking at and responding to situations in your environment.

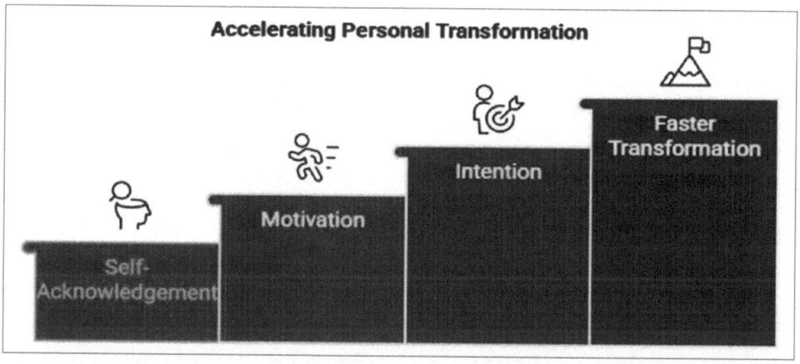

At this point, you are still learning, applying and absorbing new ways of being. The new behaviours will take some time to become automatic and ingrained in your daily routine.

The absorption to happen seamlessly requires consistency and repetition. Begin with small, manageable changes and slowly increase the pace.

Self-acknowledgement, motivation and intention propels the journey of transformation at a faster pace.

In case you miss out on a new behaviour, be kind and understanding with yourself. Quickly come back to your new set of behaviours!

10 RECAP

In the preceding portions of the book, I have shared in detail the Transformative Transitions Framework and how awakening awareness and self-assessment prime professionals to act for their personal and professional growth. I have also explored **Executive Coaching and Mentoring** — its definitions, benefits backed by research findings, and the myths surrounding it. This section illustrated how coaching and mentoring can enable professionals to rise, evolve, and accelerate their journey of self-elevation with the guidance of an Executive Coach and Mentor.

Now you have 2 choices:

Either

You can take my help to coach and mentor senior professionals in your organization, and together, we can work to find solutions to the challenges you face.

OR

Choose to use your internal resources to tackle these challenges on your own. This route is always available, but remember: without a compass, the journey may take longer.

If you've chosen Path One, I'd be glad to connect. You can schedule a one-on-one meeting with me at **manjulacoaching@gmail.com.**

Remember, the path of transformation begins with a single decision—to act. Whether you choose external guidance or internal exploration, what matters most is not delaying the journey. The world is evolving fast, and so must we. The earlier you start, the further you'll go.

❖ ❖ ❖ ❖

11 ACHIEVEMENTS

As you reach the conclusion of your executive coaching journey, take a moment to pause, breathe, and reflect because **this is your moment to celebrate.**

Executive coaching is not just about setting goals; it's about evolving through the process of achieving them. With every session, you've taken bold steps forward—tackling real-world challenges, uncovering deeper self-awareness, expanding your thinking, and refining your leadership approach. Each action you took, each perspective you shifted, and every breakthrough you experienced has brought you closer to becoming the best version of yourself.

By the end of your coaching sessions, you'll notice the transformation not just in outcomes, but in **how you think, respond, and lead.** Whether it's improved team dynamics, higher emotional resilience, greater clarity in decision-making, or renewed confidence—you now carry tools and strategies that will serve you for life.

Your coach has served as a bridge, helping you move from your **current state** to your **desired state,** but remember you did the work. You dared to explore. You chose growth. You showed up.

So now, as you look back at the goals you once wrote down and see how far you've come—smile. You've earned every bit of it.

This is your victory. Own it.

Celebrate your milestones, however big or small. Let this not be the end, but a beginning of a renewed journey filled with purpose, power, and progress.

Let's celebrate! Hurray! The transformation is real, and it's just the start.

❖ ❖ ❖ ❖

12 Case Studies

She Found Her Voice Again

Not long ago, I had the opportunity to work with a senior professional from a mid-sized organization (original name kept confidential). She came to me feeling overwhelmed and under confident, even though she had more than a decade of experience in her field. On the outside, everything seemed fine. But inside, she felt stuck and unsure of how to move forward in her career.

In our first session, I remember she said, "I feel like I've lost my voice in meetings. I know what I want to say, but I just can't speak up." We started small. We worked on self-awareness, understanding what was holding her back, and slowly created a space where she could open up without fear of being judged.

Session by session, she started gaining clarity and confidence. She started speaking up more, taking decisions faster, and even giving honest feedback to her team, something she used to avoid earlier. I saw her mindset shift from "Can I really do this?" to "I've got this."

By the end of our journey together, not only did she take up a bigger role in her organization, but she also became a mentor to others around her. Her growth made me smile not because of the success alone, but because she believed in herself again.

These are the moments that remind me why I do what I do. Coaching isn't magic; it's a journey. And I feel blessed to walk alongside professionals in that journey.

A Conversation That Opened Doors

It was December 2024, and I had the chance to attend a summit in Gurugram, Haryana. That's where I met Mr. Mittal (original name kept confidential). Our first interaction was quite easy-going. He struck me as very approachable and genuine, not at all the typical "serious businessman" persona that I often come across. His energy was friendly, and there was something very down-to-earth about him.

We got talking over coffee during a break. We discussed the usual topics — business, the summit, and the industry. But as we continued chatting, he revealed something that made me pause. He spoke about how despite his professional success, he had begun to feel like his career was stagnating. "It feels like I'm doing all the right things, but somehow, it's just not giving me the satisfaction it used to," he said, looking thoughtful.

I could tell there was more to his words than just professional burnout. There was a deeper, unspoken frustration. He didn't seem unhappy, but there was a certain disconnection in his words. I suggested that he take some time to reflect on his journey and consider executive coaching. I could tell he wasn't completely convinced at first, but he agreed to give it a shot.

A few weeks after the summit, Mr. Mittal reached out, asking for a one-on-one coaching session. During our first session, we explored the root causes of his dissatisfaction. He was an accomplished leader, but his focus was largely on his team and the company's needs, leaving little space for his own development. We worked on understanding what truly drove him and began developing a plan to realign his personal goals with his career.

As the sessions progressed, a noticeable change began. He started taking more time for himself — to think, reflect, and make decisions that weren't just based on external expectations but also on what he wanted to achieve for himself. The most surprising transformation came when he started delegating more, trusting his team, and allowing himself to focus on high-level strategic decisions. This shift not only improved his own work-life balance but also had a positive effect on his team's morale and productivity.

A few months into the coaching process, Mr. Mittal told me, "I'm seeing things from a new perspective now. It's not just about what I achieve at work, but how I feel about it. I'm doing better, and my team is responding to that change." It was a gratifying moment, knowing that coaching had helped him rediscover a sense of purpose and balance in both his professional and personal life.

The Unlikely Turnaround

In March 2025, I attended a networking event in Mumbai, where I met a young woman named Priya (original name kept confidential). She had just been promoted to lead a small team at a digital marketing company. At first, she seemed friendly and confident, but I could sense she was a little unsure about how to manage the new role.

Priya shared with me that despite being great at her job, she was facing trouble getting her team excited and motivated about the projects. She felt like they weren't really listening to her ideas, and their performance wasn't improving. It was clear that she was doing her best, but something wasn't clicking with her team. She was starting to feel stuck.

I suggested we do some coaching sessions to help her out. We decided to focus on one thing: communication. Priya had a lot of good ideas but wasn't always able to articulate them in a way that her team could connect with. She was speaking more like a technical expert and less like a leader who understood her team's needs. This made the team feel disconnected, and as a result, they weren't as engaged or productive.

We started working on how she could communicate better. I encouraged Priya to listen more to her team and to ask them questions about what they thought and felt. She also needed to make sure she was being clear and not using too much technical language that the team couldn't understand. The more Priya listened and communicated openly with her team, the more trust and respect she built with them.

Over time, Priya's confidence grew. She wasn't just giving orders anymore; she was leading in a way that made her team feel heard and valued. Her team began to open up more, share ideas, and work better together. Their productivity started to improve, and the atmosphere in the office became more positive.

By the end of our coaching, Priya was able to look back and say, "I never knew how important it was to just listen to my team and communicate clearly. Now I feel much more confident, and my team is much more motivated."

What I learned from Priya's story is that leadership isn't always about having all the answers or being the smartest person in the room. Sometimes, it's about understanding people, having good conversations, and showing that you care about their thoughts and feelings. Priya's success came from building trust with her team, and that made all the difference.

I could go on and on, sharing numerous stories like this, as I've had the privilege of witnessing many such transformations. The pages could be filled with one case study after another, but here's the thing – I don't want this book to feel like just another theoretical guide. This isn't just for those already in leadership roles, but for everyone, no matter where they are in their journey. And honestly, the whole process of reflecting on these moments has been incredibly valuable for me!

❖ ❖ ❖ ❖